Plants

Roots

Patricia Whitehouse

Raintree

www.raintreepublishers.co.uk
Visit our website to find out more information about **Raintree** books.

To order:
☎ Phone 44 (0) 1865 888112
🗎 Send a fax to 44 (0) 1865 314091
💻 Visit the Raintree Bookshop at **www.raintreepublishers.co.uk** to browse our catalogue and order online.

First published in Great Britain by Raintree, Halley Court, Jordan Hill, Oxford OX2 8EJ, part of Harcourt Education.
Raintree is a registered trademark of Harcourt Education Ltd.

Editorial: Nick Hunter and Diyan Leake
Design: Sue Emerson (HL-US) and Joanna Sapwell (www.tipani.co.uk)
Picture Research: Amor Montes de Oca (HL-US)
Production: Jonathan Smith

Originated by Dot Gradations
Printed and bound in China by South China Printing Company

ISBN 1 844 21066 9
07 06 05 04 03
10 9 8 7 6 5 4 3 2 1

British Library Cataloguing in Publication Data
Whitehouse, Patricia
Roots
575.5'4
A full catalogue record for this book is available from the British Library.

Acknowledgements
The publishers would like to thank the following for permission to reproduce photographs:
Amor Montes de Oca pp. 1, 16; Color Pic, Inc. pp. 12R, 21 (E. R. Degginger); Craig Mitchrlldyer pp. 18, 19; Dwight Kuhn pp. 4, 6, 8, 10, 11, 12L, 13, 14L, 22, 23 (root hairs, stem, taproot), 24, back cover (root hairs); Lynn M. Stone p. 20; Rick Wetherbee pp. 15, 17, back cover (ginger root); Visuals Unlimited pp. 5L (R. Ashley), 5R (Carol & Don Spencer), 7 (Marc Epstein), 9 (Jerome Wexler), 14R (John Cunningham).

Cover photograph of plants and their roots reproduced with permission of Dwight Kuhn

Every effort has been made to contact copyright holders of any material reproduced in this book. Any omissions will be rectified in subsequent printings if notice is given to the publishers.

Some words are shown in bold, **like this.** You can find them in the glossary on page 23.

Contents

What are roots?

stem

root

Roots are parts of plants that are under the **stem**.

Most roots are underground.

4

Some roots are in water.

Some roots are in air.

Why do plants have roots?

root hairs

Roots store food for plants.

The **root hairs** soak up the water plants need.

Roots hold plants in place so they do not fall over.

Where do roots come from?

seed

root

Roots come from **seeds**.

Roots are the first of a plant part that comes out of a seed.

leaf

stem

root

Some plants can grow roots from their **stems**.

Other plants can grow roots from their leaves.

How big are roots?

Roots come in many sizes.

Grass roots are short and thin.

Some roots are long.

Big, long roots like carrots are called **taproots**.

How many roots can a plant have?

radish

maize roots

Some plants have one root.

Some plants have lots of roots.

Some plants may have hundreds
of roots.

What kind of shape do roots have?

Some roots are round.

Some roots look like hair.

This is the root of a ginger plant.

It is shaped like a person!

What colours do roots come in?

Roots can be many colours.

Some roots are red.

Sweet potatoes are orange.

How do people use roots?

People use roots for food.

When you eat carrots, you are eating roots.

We eat some roots raw.

We bake or fry other roots before we eat them.

How do animals use roots?

Animals use roots for food, too.

Animals can hide in the roots
of trees.

They use roots to make their homes.

Quiz

Can you remember what these kinds of roots are called?

Look for the answers on page 24.

?

?

Glossary

root hairs
parts of roots that are so small,
they look like hair

stem
part of a plant where the leaves
and flowers grow

taproot
big main root

Index

Answers to quiz on page 22

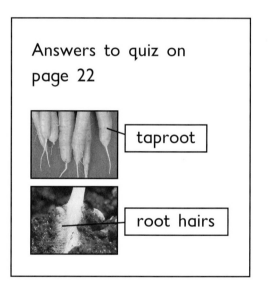

taproot

root hairs

Titles in the Plants series include:

Hardback   1 844 21064 2

Hardback   1 844 21065 0

Hardback   1 844 21066 9

Hardback   1 844 21067 7

Hardback   1 844 21068 5

Hardback   1 844 21069 3

Find out about the other titles in this series on our website www.raintreepublishers.co.uk